How Not to Kill
YOUR PLANT

Albatros

1. Basics of care

Getting to know: houseplants 4
Glossary 6
Houseplants up close 7
My room with and without
houseplants 8
What you will need 10
Soil and pots 12
Water and watering 14
Light and heat 16
Choosing the right
houseplant for you 18

2. Encyclopedia of houseplants

Peace lily 20
Fiddle-leaf fig 21
Monstera 22
String of hearts 23
Burgundy shamrock 24
Chinese money plant 25
Jade 26
Cactus 27
Aloe vera 28
Umbrella plant 29
Moss ball 30
Palm 31
Polka dot begonia 32
Prayer plant 33
ZZ plant 34
Snake plant 35

3. Cultivation practice

Buying your houseplant 36
Your houseplant
throughout the year 38
Transplanting 42
Trimming 44
Propagation 45
Expectation vs. reality 48
Problems 50
Pests 52
You're a proper carer
at last! 54

Getting to know: houseplants

Do you like the scents, colors, and variety of nature? Did you know that green is calming, just like being in the countryside? That's right: in the country, your mind is calmer and relieves itself of tension and worries. No wonder, then, that people fill their homes with plants. Why not bring a piece of nature home with you? We refer to plants that live in our homes as **houseplants**. Most of these are exotic plants whose origin makes them used to conditions rather different from the ones where we live. So, in order for them to grow well, we must create an environment where they feel at home.

Let's learn how to do this together.

This book will help you in your early days as a cultivator of plants, and beyond. In fact, it will continue to be of use to you when you are quite experienced.

It contains all you need to know, plus lots of extra tips. It will teach you what to notice, how to care for your plants from day to day, how to choose the right plant, and what to do if you get into difficulties. There is no catchall guide to successful plant care. And not even following procedures to the letter will guarantee that your plants will grow as you wish them to. Caring for houseplants requires a combination of knowledge, experience, and empathy. In short, plants need to be monitored to ensure that they are reacting well to your care. But one thing is for sure: your perseverance with them will be rewarded.

Each yellow box contains basic information on a given topic.

....

A circle with a number **5** in it refers you to another page of this book, where you will find more related information.

....

In this book we work with a limited number of plants. It doesn't matter at all if your houseplant is not among our choices. Although there are many plant species, principles of care tend to be much the same for each of them.

....

This book is divided into three parts. In the first, you will learn about the basic conditions in which plants should be kept. In the second, you will choose a plant from the encyclopedia of houseplants. In the third, you will learn about plant care throughout the year.

....

The encyclopedia of houseplants is easy to find, thanks to the green borders on the pages of that section.

Glossary

When reading this book and tending your plants, you will encounter various terms. Here you can find the most basic ones explained. If you can't remember what they mean, turn to this page for a reminder.

Cutting – a piece cut from a plant (e.g., a leaf, branch, or part of the stem) for placing in a glass of water or moist soil, where it will take root, after which it can be grown into a new plant.

Dew-drop moistening – a type of watering by which we wet the surface of a houseplant's leaves when they need to increase humidity. Applied with a sprayer.

Dormancy – period during which a plant's vital functions are slower, with the result that it grows very slowly or not at all. Tends to occur in late autumn or winter.

Drain – a layer of pebbles or balls of expanded clay at the bottom of the pot, which drains excess water from the roots. A protection against overwatering.

Fertilizer – nutrients for plants, applied in the form of sticks or mixed with water. May be chemically produced or come from natural sources.

Growing season – period during which conditions are favorable for plant growth. Usually occurs in spring and summer, when there's more light and heat, so that the plants grow faster and create new leaves.

Houseplant – a plant tended at home, indoors. Most houseplants are of exotic origin and have decorative flowers and/or leaves.

Humidity – concentration of water vapor in the air. Some plants require high humidity. We increase humidity by dewdrop moistening, showering, or the use of an air humidifier. The greater the number of plants in an indoor space, the higher the humidity in that space. Dry air is a threat to plant health, especially in the warm season.

Location – place where a houseplant is kept. Conditions should be suitable for its species, not least in terms of light intensity.

Substrate – soil mix in which a plant will thrive. The substrate provides it with nutrients and water retained from watering.

Succulent – a plant whose stem and leaves store water, allowing it to survive long periods of drought. Its leaves and stem are thick and fleshy. Stonecrops and aloes are common houseplant succulents.

Summer care – keeping indoor plants outside (e.g., on a balcony or patio) in summertime so that they grow better and are more resistant in wintertime. We move them outside only when temperatures have stabilized and there is no danger of frost, in the second half of May at the earliest.

Watering – giving plants water in accordance with their needs. Tools for increasing plant moisture include a watering can, a shower, and a dew-drop moistener.

Winter care – caring for indoor plants in wintertime by moving them to cooler areas of the home (e.g., a hall or landing) and watering them less.

Houseplants up close

Like other plants, houseplants are composed of three main parts: **roots**, **leaves**, and **stem**. In the wild, plants produce flowers and fruit; it is unusual for houseplants to do so, as only certain species flower.

The three main plant parts vary in appearance, in terms of shape, texture, and size. As the case may be, however, each has its special function, without which the plant would not survive.

The **flower** produces fruit and seeds, which in the wild serve for reproduction.

Leaves absorb heat and light, vaporize water, and help the houseplant gain energy for growth.

The **stem** is the plant's main support. Nutrients pass through it to all parts of the plant.

The plant obtains water and nutrients from the soil through the **roots**.

My room without houseplants

You may be wondering about the point of getting a houseplant. Your room is nice and cozy without one, isn't it? Besides, plant care is a complicated matter, so why make more work for yourself? Isn't it better to play? But let's say you do decide to get a houseplant. How will it make your room different?

My room with houseplants

With houseplants, your room suddenly becomes even cozier. As well as looking good, many houseplants purify and humidify the air, making it easier for you to sleep and breathe. In short, you will feel a little like you do in the countryside—relaxed and contented. But if plant care is to become your hobby, you should know that it is habit-forming: you won't be satisfied with only one or two plants. Another benefit of this pastime is that it is fun and creative. Why not make the plants in your room into a small jungle, hang them from the ceiling, or use them to liven up a boring shelf or windowsill?

What you will need

Every keeper of houseplants needs patience and determination, plus a few other things. These things include tools. It is OK to get some tools when the need arises, but you will need others from the start. All your needs will be met by a flower shop or garden center, where you can choose from many materials, sizes, and designs. The main thing is, your tools should be the right ones for you and your plants, making caring for your plants as easy as possible.

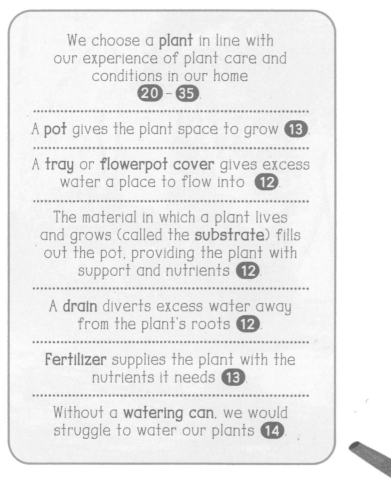

We choose a **plant** in line with our experience of plant care and conditions in our home **20** – **35**.

A **pot** gives the plant space to grow **13**.

A **tray** or **flowerpot cover** gives excess water a place to flow into **12**.

The material in which a plant lives and grows (called the **substrate**) fills out the pot, providing the plant with support and nutrients **12**.

A **drain** diverts excess water away from the plant's roots **12**.

Fertilizer supplies the plant with the nutrients it needs **13**.

Without a **watering can**, we would struggle to water our plants **14**.

support sticks

pot   tray

drain   sprayer

seeds   gloves

knife   scissors   rake

watering cans

We use a **cloth** to wipe dust from the leaves.

A **knife** and **scissors** are used to shape plants or remove old or damaged parts **44**. Tools must be clean, to safeguard against the spread of dirt, bacteria, or pests. Special garden scissors or plant clippers are best.

string

We use a **sprayer** on plants that need dew, since the leaves on their surface must be moist **15**.

Gloves make it easier to repot plants **42**. They also protect the hands against dirt and injury.

flowerpot cover

A **trowel** and a **rake** make work with soil easier. Not only do they keep our hands clean, but they also place the soil exactly where it is needed.

cloth

String and **support sticks** help plants to grow as they should.

trowel

plant   fertilizer   substrate

Soil and pots

To successfully cultivate a houseplant, choosing the right pot and an appropriate substrate is essential. The plant takes nutrients from the substrate, while the pot provides space for its roots to grow. The plant's conditions should be as close as possible to those in which it lives in the wild. Pot size affects the amount of soil and water available to the plant, thus determining how happy it will be.

A **flowerpot cover** is more than just a nice decoration; above all, it is a functioning tray for collecting excess water. The cover should not be too tight: there must be at least one centimeter between it and the pot.

Pot size and material are important: as they define the plant's living space, they have a big influence on its growth. It is not always the case that a bigger pot is better.

The size of the tray must correspond to that of the pot. It should be at least as broad as the pot's top edge.

Different plants thrive in different substrates (i.e., soil compositions).

When we don't know which soil to choose, we use a universal substrate for houseplants.

flowerpot covers

expanded clay balls

A **drain** is a layer at the bottom of the pot that ensures that excess water drains away, thus protecting the roots from rot. We use one with all plants watered from the top **15**. Balls of expanded clay are a popular drain; pebbles, pieces of glass, and a broken flowerpot can also be used as a drain.

A **substrate** fills out the pot, creating a "living space" for the plant from which it receives nutrients. Some houseplants require a substrate of special composition; this can be bought ready-made or mixed at home. It is good to change the substrate regularly, because after a year or so it no longer contains very many nutrients and loses its ability to retain water.

Fertilizer nourishes plants. It comes in liquid, powder, and stick form. When administering a dose, we always follow the instructions on the pack. Fertilizer is mostly applied in spring and summer.

A **tray** collects water that the soil in the pot does not have time to absorb after watering. We pour this excess water away. With some plants, we water only into the tray **15**.

fertilizer

trays

universal substrate

special substrates

flowerpots

The **pot** must have a hole in the bottom for the outflow of excess water, and it must be the right size. If the pot is too small, the plant will lack space for growth. If it is too large, rooting will require a lot of energy, thus slowing down growth.

We choose the **pot's material** based on the type of plant and how we will water it. **Terracotta** lets in more water, thus reducing the risk of overwatering and root rot. A **plastic** pot holds more water, making it better if we forget to water the plant.

Water and watering

For good care, it is essential to give plants the right amount of water at the right time. Good plant-watering is like alchemy—some plants need watering occasionally, but others require it practically every day. In addition, our spring and summer watering practices are very different from our winter ones. We water most plants from the top of the pot, but some require water only in the tray. For this reason, it is important to know your plants and the conditions that suit them. To claim something like "We must water the plants on Wednesdays" is nonsense.

How often and how much we water our plants depends on how much light and heat **16** they have.

If by sticking a finger in the substrate we find the soil to be dry, it is time to water the plant.

Don't water your plants in the evening or when the sun is at its strongest.

Use settled water so that it is at room temperature.

Plants need more water in spring and summer than in autumn and winter.

For watering, it is best to use **settled water** at room temperature. Cold or hot water might give a plant temperature shock. Tap water contains chlorine and mineral deposits, which are harmful to plants, but when the water settles for at least a day, the toxins are released and the water is safe. So we should prepare water for our plants in advance, in special containers.

The **watering can** for your houseplants should have a **long thin funnel**, allowing you to reach the plant's stem as well as just the pot.

watering can with long funnel

settled water

sprayer

In spring and summer we can **shower** our plants with lukewarm water. As well as giving them a good wetting, it will clear their leaves of dust, thereby allowing them to breathe better. Showering is also good protection against pests **52**.

We water most houseplants **into the pot from the top**. Excess water flows into the tray, from where we pour it away.
We water succulents and plants sensitive to stem and leaf rot **directly into the tray**; the plant will take the water from the tray itself. Such plants must not have a drain in the pot, as this would prevent the water from reaching the plant.

Plants of tropical origin, which are used to high humidity, love to be **dewdrop moistened** with a sprayer. Their leaves should not be made so wet that the water drips from them.

Light and heat

As well as water, soil, and air, every plant needs light and heat. Without them, it would cease to grow and start to wither. Needs for light vary from one plant to the next, however. For this reason, we can't put a houseplant wherever we wish, or where we happen to have space. We must find the right spot for it, so light conditions are crucial. They are divided into four categories, depending on light intensity: direct sunlight, diffuse light, partial shade, and full shade. We position our plant according to its specific needs. Sometimes we must work with a chosen location—e.g., by more intensive watering, or by ensuring that the plant is not in a draft or too close to a radiator. As no one place in the home offers the same conditions all year round, we should expect to move the plant from one place to another.

Partial shade is usually found away from windows, where there is little direct sunlight. It is also found near poorly lit windows (typically in a north-facing location).

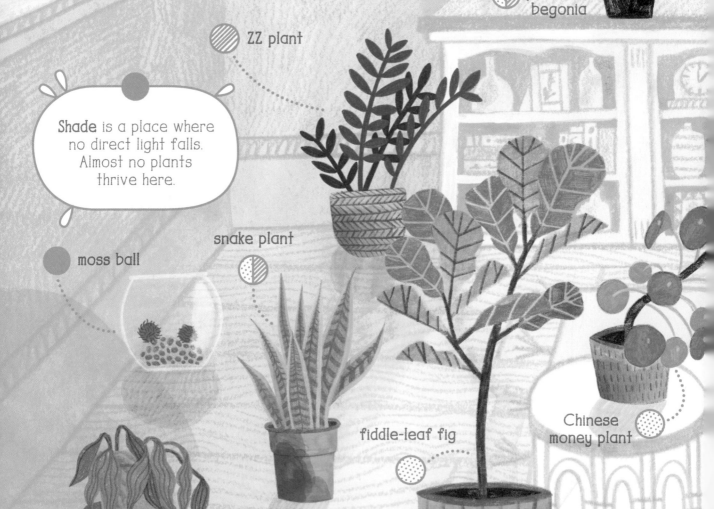

polka dot begonia

ZZ plant

Shade is a place where no direct light falls. Almost no plants thrive here.

moss ball

snake plant

fiddle-leaf fig

Chinese money plant

16

string
of hearts

prayer plant

palm

jade

umbrella plant

cactus

aloe
vera

We find **direct light** mostly
by a window where the
sun shines for most of
the day (typically in
a south-facing location).
Such a place is suitable
for succulents and tough
houseplants with fleshy
leaves.

Don't underestimate the importance
of location. It determines how well
our plant grows, and how to care
for it.

When choosing a plant, consider the
point of the compass towards which
your room faces. Light intensity
also depends on distance from the
window and the floor you live on.

A change of location is often
necessary before winter, when
there is less light.

Don't move your plants too often:
it is not good for them.

Don't place plants too close
to radiators: they dislike dry air
and changing temperatures.

We tend to find **diffuse light** by
windows into which the sun shines with
less intensity, or only for part of the
day (typically in west- or east-facing
locations). We also find it in places near
windows where the plant can "see the sky".
It's suitable for most houseplants.

Choosing the right houseplant for you

Now that you know what a plant needs to grow well, the crucial moment is approaching—you will soon be choosing your own. Before you make your choice, however, you should ask yourself a few questions.

What do I have to offer?
Think about the conditions and care you can offer a plant. Do you have enough space for it? Are the light and temperature in your room right for the plant you are considering? If you have a pet, you must be sure that it will not nibble at the plant, which could be dangerous for its health. When choosing a plant, you should think about how much time you are prepared to give. Some plants need more care than others.

What can I expect from my houseplant?
Do you want to fill your room with plants, or will one or two be enough for now? Do you want a really big one, or would you prefer one with leaves of interesting shape and color? Although knowing what you want is important, you should bear in mind that the more plants you have, the more demands they will make on your time. Are you truly able to give them the attention they need?

How experienced am I as a carer for plants?
Are you a beginner, or do you have some experience caring for plants? If the former, you would do well to learn the basics of plant care on a plant that doesn't make many demands. If the latter, or if you are bold in your approach, why not try some more demanding species? Be aware that even the most experienced carer gets things wrong sometimes. It is important not to be discouraged by failures.

As there are hundreds of types of houseplants, you have a lot to choose from! In the pages to come, you will get to know some of the basic, most popular species. So, welcome to our **encyclopedia of houseplants**!

In the entry for each plant you will find information on intensity of watering, the most suitable location, demands of care, plus other practical advice and points of interest.

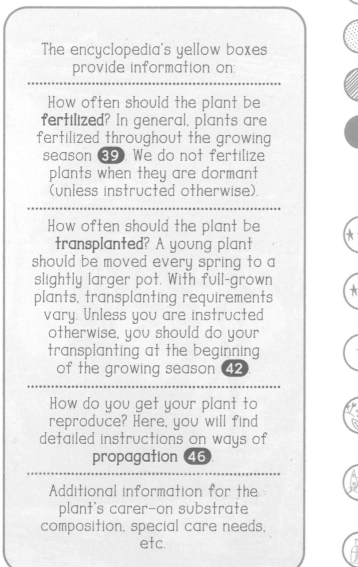

The encyclopedia's yellow boxes provide information on:

How often should the plant be **fertilized**? In general, plants are fertilized throughout the growing season **39**. We do not fertilize plants when they are dormant (unless instructed otherwise).

How often should the plant be **transplanted**? A young plant should be moved every spring to a slightly larger pot. With full-grown plants, transplanting requirements vary. Unless you are instructed otherwise, you should do your transplanting at the beginning of the growing season **42**.

How do you get your plant to reproduce? Here, you will find detailed instructions on ways of **propagation 46**.

Additional information for the plant's carer–on substrate composition, special care needs, etc.

Intensity and frequency of watering

 water a lot and often

 water regularly and in moderation

 water regularly, but less often and to a lesser extent

Ideal light intensity

 direct light

 diffuse light

 partial shade

 full shade

Demands of care

 for experts = plants that place high demands on conditions and care

 for advanced carers = plants that place moderate demands on conditions and care

 for beginners = resilient plants that make low demands

Flowers

Unsuitable for pets: can cause health issues. Keep out of reach of small children.

Needs dewdrop moistening

Peace lily

SPATIPHYLLUM

- The peace lily is suitable for rooms where the air should be kept pure: it absorbs harmful substances and even some poisonous gases.
- It comes from the jungles of Central America, so it likes relatively high humidity. For this reason, when it is not in flower, use a dewdrop moistener on it, open its leaves with a damp cloth, or shower it.
- Be aware that it is toxic. A nibble at its leaves could give a pet tummy trouble or even poisoning. If juice from the leaves gets on your skin, you may get a nasty rash.
- From spring to autumn, it produces white flowers reminiscent of arrow quivers.

A great-looking plant that purifies the air

Fertilize 1x in 2 weeks.

Repot rarely, e.g. 1x in 3 years.

Propagate by division.

The substrate should always be moist, but there should be no standing water in the tray.

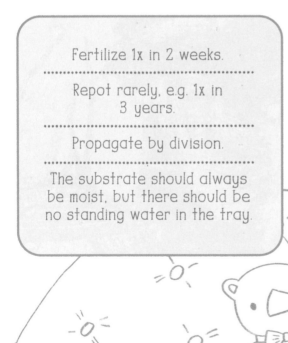

Fiddle-leaf fig

FICUS LYRATA

- The fiddle-leaf fig is easily identifiable by its violin- or lyre-shaped leaves. A thriving plant will grow to a height of up to 10 feet.
- The fiddle-leaf is one of many fig species. Also common, and easier to care for, are the Benjamin fig (whose leaves are small) and the rubber fig (whose leaves are large and leathery).
- Figs are very popular houseplants. They can be shaped, are easy to propagate, and when treated well will give enjoyment for many years.
- They love dewdrop moistening and showering. Their substrate should be neither overwatered nor allowed to dry out. It should be permeable, and the pot should have a drain.
- If you wish for your fig to grow outwards, grasp the leaves at its sides to get it to gain in volume. Cuttings can be taken for propagation.

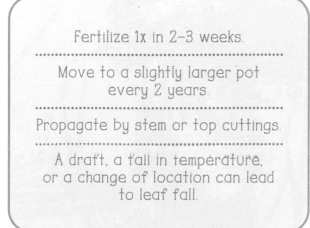

Fertilize 1x in 2–3 weeks.

Move to a slightly larger pot every 2 years.

Propagate by stem or top cuttings.

A draft, a fall in temperature, or a change of location can lead to leaf fall.

It will grow to be taller than you

21

Monstera

MONSTERA DELICIOSA

- The tropical monstera is a big hit among house-plants. It is characterized by leaves with holes in the blade. These leaves can be as large as plates. The plant can be over 6 feet tall.
- There are several species of monstera. You could start with a smaller one before moving on to one of truly monstrous proportions.
- Runners that grow from the stem are known as aerial roots. The plant absorbs moisture and nutrients from the air. Aerial roots cling to a support as they grow upwards, so put a stick in the pot for them to climb.
- If a monstera doesn't get enough light, its leaves will not acquire their characteristic holes.
- In the wild, it produces white flowers. As a houseplant, it flowers in rare cases only.

Your own bit of jungle in the living room

Fertilize 1x in 2 weeks.

Do not transplant until the pot is filled with roots.

Propagate by a cutting from which an aerial root is growing.

It likes dewdrop moistening and showering, and it will benefit from being wiped by a cloth.

String of hearts

CEROPEGIA WOODII

- This plant's overhanging branches filled with heart-shaped leaves are most striking when hung by a window in a sunny place.
- It thrives in similar conditions to those favored by succulents: it likes dry air, and it dislikes moisture. It requires plenty of light. It should be watered only when the substrate is drying.
- It produces tuberous purple flowers in summer, when we water it more than usual.
- A string of hearts is unlikely to be attacked by pests. If healthy, it is highly resistant to them.

A plant pot full of hearts

Fertilize 1x per month.

Repot every 2–3 years.

Propagate by taking cuttings or tubers.

It thrives in a substrate for cacti.

Burgundy shamrock

OXALIS TRIANGULARIS

- The burgundy shamrock is an undemanding houseplant with unusual purple coloring. It reacts to light: in daytime, its leaves spread out, while at night they close to store energy for growth.
- It is watered from the bottom into a tray, but only when its substrate has dried out. It reacts badly to overwatering.
- Some other species of Oxalis have green coloring and resemble the four-leaf clover. There is no need to moisten the leaves; dust can be showered away.

Houseplant with butterfly wings

Fertilize 1x in 2 weeks.

Repot in spring, but only if needed.

Propagate by division or tubers.

Even when almost dried-out, it will sprout new leaves after watering.

Chinese money plant

PILEA PEPEROMIOIDES

- The Chinese money plant is a very attractive and popular houseplant. It is notable for its splendid, unusual round leaves.
- As its stem leans towards the sun, it should be turned from time to time so that it remains straight and doesn't lose its shape.
- A thriving Chinese money plant will produce a small "baby" next to the mother plant. This can be cut away and grown into a new plant.
- Water only when the surface of the substrate is dry.
- If its water is too hard, the undersides of its leaves develop white spots. When this occurs, the plant should be watered with boiled water.
- Small, white-yellow flowers appear in exceptional cases.
- From China, it is said to bring wealth.

Fertilize 1x in 2 weeks.

Repot in spring, but only if needed.

Propagate by offsets ("babies") or stem cuttings.

Leaves will curl in strong light or excessive heat.

Grow yourself some money

Jade

CRASSULA OVATA

Houseplant with great staying power

- There are several crassula species, all characterized by strong, fleshy, pillowy leaves.
- Jades are resilient, long-lasting house-plants that can be shaped by regular trimming, in the manner of the bonsai.
- Water them rarely; 1x in 2 weeks is enough. As they dislike overwatering, it is important that they be given a drain. A substrate for cacti is ideal, too, for jades.
- For summer, they like to be moved into the fresh air, like to a balcony or garden. When dormant, they should be kept in a cooler room.
- They need plenty of light. If deprived of it, their leaves will yellow and fall.
- They grow very slowly but will last for many years. Older jade plants may flower, but not always.

Fertilize at least 1x in 2 months.
....
Transplant when the roots become too big for the pot.
....
Propagate by leaf or stem cuttings.
....
A succulent, it can tolerate drought and extreme heat.

Cactus

CACTACEAE

- Cacti are a very large, varied family of plants with a very tough stem and leaves transformed into spines. Species vary in terms of shape, size, and demands of care. You should always check the needs of your particular cactus.
- One advantage of cacti is that they withstand long-lasting drought and heat, making them quite easy to care for.
- Unlike some houseplants, most cacti prefer to be watered in the evening, always into the tray.
- Water sparingly: overwatered cacti soon begin to rot.
- Some cactus species produce multicolored flowers.
- Before winter, cacti should be placed in a cooler room.

Watch your fingers!

Fertilize max. 1x per month with special fertilizer for cacti.

In spring or summer, transplant to a terracotta pot. Do not water for 2 weeks after repotting.

Propagate by offsets.

It needs an airy, permeable substrate, like one with sand.

Aloe vera

ALOE VERA

- Aloe vera is more than just decorative. Because of its healing powers, it is used to make cosmetics, ointments, and drinks. The pulp of its leaves can be used for the fast-acting treatment of scratches and sunburn.
- To thrive, it needs well-drained soil and plenty of light and heat.
- It does not cope well with overwatering, developing black spots when exposed to it.
- When transplanting, take offsets from the mother plant and set each in its own pot.

Family doctor

Fertilize 1x per month.

Transplant when it outgrows its pot.

Propagate by offsets or leaf cuttings.

An undemanding succulent, it copes well with drought and low humidity.

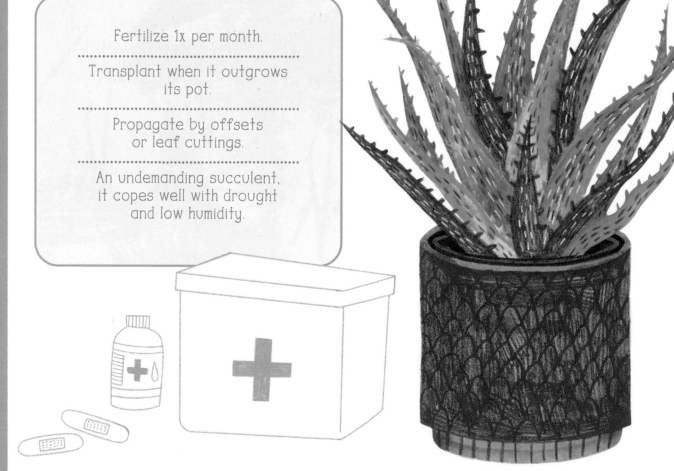

Umbrella plant

SCHEFFLERA ARBORICOLA

- The umbrella plant is a popular houseplant with umbrella-like leaves. Not only is it pleasant to look at, but it also purifies the air and absorbs chemicals. Its leaves are poisonous to pets, however.
- Water frequently but only when the surface of the substrate is dry.
- It thrives in an acidic substrate with peat in it.
- To ensure that your umbrella plant grows straight, and the stem does not break under the weight of the leaves, it should be supported by a stick attached to the plant.

Beware!
This beauty
is poisonous.

Fertilize 1x in 2 weeks; in winter, 1x per month.

Repot every spring.

Propagate by stem cuttings.

It is sensitive to drafts and changes in temperature.

Moss ball

CLADOPHORA AEGROPILA

- A moss ball is an unusual houseplant. Its original decorative use was in aquariums. Only later was it cultivated for display in its own right.
- A moss ball is a clump of seaweed from the cold lakes of Japan. As a houseplant, it is kept in the water of a mini-aquarium or another glass container, away from windows.
- It likes cold water. From time to time, moss balls (in their containers) might be placed in a fridge, or else ice cubes might be added to their water.
- When changing their water, rinse the moss balls carefully in running water. As you do so, squeeze and roll them in your hands—this will aerate them, helping them retain their roundness.
- Discontented moss balls may turn brown. If this happens, they should be rinsed repeatedly, placed in cold water, and kept in the shade.
- If you have a pet, you might let it drink from the moss balls' container. As the water in it is oxygenated, cats and others enjoy its taste.

Change its water every 7–10 days.

....

It can be squeezed and rolled in the hands.

....

Its propagation at home is not possible.

Houseplant or pet?

Palm

ARECACEAE

- The exotic palm evokes memories of sunshine and hot summers. Kept in the home, it can grow to an impressive size.
- There are many species of palm, and requirements in terms of light, heat, and moisture vary from one to the next. You should learn the requirements of the species you have.
- As palms have high demands regarding watering and humidity, regularly give them plenty of water. The surface of the substrate should be allowed to dry before watering.
- Palms are expert purifiers of air, making them perfect for sunny bedrooms.

Do you miss the sea?

Fertilize 1x in 2 weeks.

Transplant only when the roots become too large for the pot.

Propagate by division.

It dislikes drafts and high temperatures.

Polka dot begonia

BEGONIA MACULATA

- The polka dot begonia is the pride of every cultivator of houseplants. It stands out from other begonias by its lovely, dotted leaves. With red coloring on the undersides, they are reminiscent of wings.
- It likes high humidity but not moistening. A begonia is best placed in a bowl of damp pebbles. The vaporizing water will moisten the plant's surroundings.
- Choose your location very carefully—direct light could burn the leaves, while a draft may cause leaf fall.
- In the growing season, it produces white-pink flowers.
- Begonias should be regularly checked for pests, as they are highly susceptible to them.

A model among houseplants

In the flowering season, fertilize 1x in 2 weeks; otherwise, fertilize 1x per month.

Repot every spring.

Propagate by top cuttings.

Brown leaves are a sign of too little water; yellowing is a sign of overwatering.

Prayer plant

MARANTHA LEUCONEURA FASCINATOR

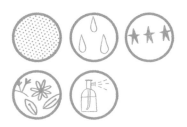

- Native to the rainforest, the various maranta species are very popular houseplants. They are characterized by beautiful patterns on the leaves and high care demands.
- For experienced cultivators only, the prayer plant requires high humidity and a constant temperature all year round. It likes showering and moistening.
- Water your prayer plant so that its substrate is always damp. You should empty excess water from its tray: the roots should not be in water.
- As it has a shallow root system, it should be placed in a short pot.
- It gets its name from the way it folds its leaves like hands at prayer. It does this in the evening or in weak light.

> Fertilize 1x in 2 weeks; in winter, fertilize 1x per month.
> ....
> Repot every two years.
> ....
> Propagate by division.
> ....
> Leaves will curl if given too little water.

Attractive to both plant fans and pets

ZZ plant

ZAMIOCULCAS ZAMIIFOLIA

- The ZZ is a resilient plant suitable for absolute beginners. It can cope with dry air, an over-dry substrate, and a dearth of light.
- It comes from Madagascar and is characterized by firm, glossy leaves that grow out of the substrate.
- It benefits from occasional dewdrop moistening, and it also likes to be showered. You should take care not to overwater it, however.
- Brown spots on the stem are a common sign of aging. A discontented ZZ plant will drop yellowed leaves.

Code name:
Tough Guy

Fertilize 1x per month.

Do not transplant unless there is no room in the pot; it likes to be squashed.

Propagate by division or leaf cuttings.

It will thrive in most conditions, provided it is not in direct light.

Snake plant

SANSEVIERIA TRIFASCIATA

· Originally from Africa, snake plant is an undemanding houseplant, suitable for beginners. It doesn't mind a dry environment, and unlike other houseplants it purifies the air at night.
· When watering, make sure that water doesn't get through the leaves to the rosette (plant center), as this will cause it to rot.
· It comes in various sizes and colors. For species with more colorful or variegated leaves, choose a location with more light.
· The name "snake plant" is a reference to the shape of its leaves, which resemble snakes.

Fierce
but kind

Fertilize 1x per month.
....
Transplant every 2-3 years, depending on when the roots grow through the holes in the pot.
....
Propagate by division, leaf cuttings, or offsets.

Buying your houseplant

Have you chosen the right houseplant for you? Then let's now do what we have been looking forward to from the start—let's take home our first plant! But where should we get it from?

There are many possibilities. These days, we find houseplants not only in specialist shops but also in large department and home improvement stores. With larger retailers, it pays to be cautious when buying. In particular, it is important to check that plants have not been overwatered and are not troubled by pests. In a garden center or specialist flower shop, we can be more confident that what we are buying is healthy and right for us.

Another widespread and popular option is to get your plant from another cultivator. Why not ask an aunt, your grandma, or a friend to give you a rooted cutting, or else a branch from one of their houseplants, which you could then help take root? Once you have your own plants for propagation, you can share with your friends, too—by giving cuttings as presents, for example.

Anyway, at last the time has come to try out what you have learned!

Before you buy, you should consider whether your home has the right conditions for the plant of your choice.

....

While still in the shop, you should check the plant for signs of ill health. Are there pests on it? Is there rot on the stem? Is there mold in the substrate?

....

Once you get it home, you should place the new plant "in quarantine" (i.e., away from other houseplants) and leave it there for two weeks.

....

Once quarantine is over, you should repot the plant in a new substrate before moving it to your chosen location.

Your houseplant throughout the year

When you get your plant home, you can look forward to a big change. Over time, plant care will become part of your routine, and you know already what needs to be done. But when the seasons change, how you care for your plant must change along with them. The growing season (spring and summer) alternates with the time of dormancy (autumn and winter). This means that the plant is active for a time, then inactive for a time. For the cultivator, this brings significant changes in care practices every early spring and early autumn. In short, what your plant appreciated in springtime will no longer please it in autumn. So you change its location, adjust the intensity and frequency of watering, and react to how the plant accepts these changes.

Resting plant = less active carer

Dormancy

AUTUMN AND WINTER

· Seasons when plants rest and their vital functions slow down.
· You should monitor and care for your plants, but don't overdo it.
· Above all, plants need sufficient light— which explains the need for a change of location. In most cases, in winter we move plants closer to the window, and so to the light.
· In autumn and winter the air should be humidified, as our home's heating makes it drier.
· Make sure that your plants aren't in a draft, for example while airing.
· Plants should not be repotted, showered, or (with rare exceptions) fertilized.
· Some plants benefit from winterization—e.g., being moved to a cooler room or hallway.

Growing season

SPRING AND SUMMER

- Seasons when plants have enough heat and light for growth.
- Plants become active as soon as winter is over. If they are properly cared for, they will grow very well and may even flower.
- With the coming of spring, there is suddenly a lot more light, so a change of location is called for. Plants that were close to a window in winter must be placed further away, to keep them from burning. You must consider the compass direction your room faces.
- You must give your plants more water and water them more often, because heat causes water to evaporate, and besides, the plant needs more water for its growth.
- When winter is over, you should give your plant a full service. Remove old leaves and give it a trim.
- In spring, some plants are repotted, while others remain in the same pot with some of their substrate changed to ensure the effective supply of nutrients.
- Plants should be fertilized regularly.
- Spring and summer are good for propagation.
- Many plants love being showered or placed outdoors——on a balcony, for instance.

In the lives of plants, the growing season (spring and summer) alternates with the period of dormancy (autumn and winter).

Plants require different care at different times of year.

Plants need the most work and are the most fun in spring. Spring is also the best time to get new houseplants.

If you are on vacation or away for some time, you must arrange for someone to care for your plants.

Active plant = active carer

Dormancy

WINTER

wipe
leaves

water
less

check for
pests

increase
humidity

AUTUMN

check for
pests

change
location

water
less

wipe
leaves

increase
humidity

Growing season

SPRING

check for
pests

propagate

change substrate or repot

change
location

take plant
cuttings

water more

shower

fertilize

trim

SUMMER

check for
pests

fertilize

shower

follow proper
summer care

propagate

water
more

Transplanting

Every spring witnesses a frenzy of activity among cultivators of houseplants. The growing season coincides with the transplanting season. In plant care, changing the substrate is very important: after the rigors of winter, plants need a fresh supply of energy and nutrients. Now is the time to decide which plants should be transplanted to a larger pot. The size of the pot should correspond to the size of the plant's roots. And what about the plants that will not be repotted this spring? Well, you should change the top layer of their substrate (3–6 cm): they, too, need their soil refreshed.

Tools

pruning clippers or scissors

substrate

support sticks

new plant pots

gardening gloves

Plants are transplanted in spring.

Only houseplants that need transplanting are repotted.

Fresh soil provides plants with nutrients.

It's untrue that the bigger the pot, the happier the plant. In most cases, the diameter of your chosen pot will be 2–3 cm greater than that of the plant.

Plants bought in stores, too, should be repotted–ideally not straightaway but after two weeks.

When to repot a plant?

| The roots are sticking out of the bottom of the pot. | The roots are pushing the plant upwards, out of its substrate. | It is spring, but the plant is not growing. | The plant is unstable. | There is a salty/mineral layer on the surface of the substrate. |

1. Water the plant well the day before repotting. This will make it easier to remove it from its pot.

2. Remove the plant from its pot.

3. As you carefully release the roots, remove old, excess soil from the plant.

4. Remove old, rotting roots.

5. Having selected a pot with a drainage hole and of appropriate size, wash this pot in soapy water.

6. Put a drain (e.g., a layer of expanding clay balls or pebbles) in the bottom of the pot. (Plants watered into a tray do not need a drain.)

7. Add a small layer of the new substrate.

8. Place the plant in the new pot.

9. Fill any remaining space in the pot with the new substrate.

10. Tamp the soil down gently with your fingers, ensuring that the plant is well anchored. Don't fill the pot with soil right to the top, but to 1 cm below it—you must leave space for watering.

11. Water the plant well (unless it is a cactus or succulent—in which case wait 2 weeks before watering).

12. Your plant has been potted. Hurray!

Trimming

For a houseplant to grow well and thrive, once winter is over it is necessary to trim it, thereby getting rid of dry branchlets and leaves. As well as making the plant look better, the right kind of trimming is good for growth. Unhealthy parts demand more energy, weakening the plant unnecessarily. Although it is best to trim in early spring, it does no harm to snip off a withered twig at other times of year.

Tools

pruning clippers or scissors

sharp knife

gardening gloves

Pruning a plant encourages it to grow.

Plants are trimmed in spring. The cut is made just below the node on the stem.

Work is performed with clean tools.

No more than a quarter of the plant is removed, so that there remains something to grow from.

Branchlets should be cut just below the node.

The cut should be diagonal, not straight.

When we cut off long, overhanging branchlets, the plant gets its shape.

If a whole branchlet is to be removed, the cut should be made as close as possible to the plant's stem.

A cut-off branchlet (cutting). It can be placed in water, where it will sprout roots; it can then be planted 42.

44

Propagation

You can never have too many houseplants. So cuttings, separation of offsets, and rooting are where it's at! For the keeper of houseplants, propagation is a fun experiment that requires patience. If we follow the correct procedure and give our plants time to take root, success is practically guaranteed. The result is a succession of new houseplants, which we care for in the same way as their mother plants. Propagation can be performed all year round, but the quickest and best rooting of new plants occurs in spring and summer; the process is quite lengthy in winter. There are many methods of propagation. Let us now show you the four most common ones.

Tools

pruning clippers or scissors

new plant pots

glass of water

knife

substrate

Individual species can be propagated in various ways.

Plant pieces for propagation should be taken from healthy mother plants.

Separated plant pieces can be placed in water or in a substrate to take root. In a substrate, rooting is quicker, but you must remember to keep the soil moist.

If the plant is to grow in a substrate, a plastic plant pot is used, as it retains moisture better.

The container of water with pieces for rooting should be placed in a well-lit, warm place.

Top and stem cuttings

top cutting

stem cutting

1. The cutting is made with a sharp knife or scissors just below the node (a place from which several leaves grow). Bottom leaves are removed from the cutting.

2. The cutting is placed in a glass of clean, settled water, which should be changed regularly. The cutting can then be planted in a substrate, which must be kept moist.

3. After the cutting has developed a root system, it is planted in a new pot of the appropriate size.

✓ figs, polka dot begonia, monstera, jade, creepers and hanging plants, string of hearts, umbrella plant

Leaf cuttings

1. Cut a leaf from the mother plant. Then cut the leaf into several pieces. Cuts should be made straight across towards the center of the leaf.

2. Cut-up leaf pieces should be planted in a moist substrate with the tip or upper cut pointing upwards. Otherwise, the leaf will fail to take root and will die.

3. It may take some weeks for a leaf to take root. Once roots have formed, each leaf is planted in a pot of its own. Some weeks after that, a new plant will be growing alongside the leaf. Once this is over 3 cm high, the original leaf can be cut away just above the soil.

✓ snake plant, jade, aloe vera

Division

1. Remove the plant from the pot and find the thinnest connection in the roots, where the plant should be carefully divided using scissors or a knife.

2. The plant is divided into no more than two, perhaps three, pieces, each with well-developed roots. Each piece is planted in its own pot.

✓ burgundy shamrock, peace lily, ZZ plant, prayer plant, palms, snake plant

Propagation by offsets and tubers

1. Take the plant from its pot and clean it so that the roots are clearly visible. With scissors or a knife, remove the root that connects the mother plant and the "baby."

2. If the young plant has a well-developed root system, it can be planted in its own pot straightaway. If the roots are still coming through, the plant should be placed in water, for planting only when ready.

A similar approach is used for propagation by tubers. Ball-shaped tubers form along the stem or roots of some plants (e.g., the string of hearts). For propagation, the piece of the plant with the tuber is cut away and planted in soil.

✓ Chinese money plant, snake plant, string of hearts, burgundy shamrock, aloe vera, cacti

Expectation

Houseplants are starting to get under your skin. You have chosen your favorites, and you follow the recommended procedure for looking after them. You have the basics of plant care down to a science. There is always a container of settled water in your room, and your sprayer is always at hand.

Reality

Oh no! What's that insect doing here? And why does my monstera have brown leaves? What could I have done wrong? Don't despair—problems are part and parcel of growing houseplants. Every cultivator finds that their plants are not always happy. Sometimes a poor choice in location is to blame. Sometimes the culprit is too little care, or, unbelievable as it may seem, too much (excessive watering is common). The most important thing is that every problem has a solution. So let's go and find it.

Problems

Try as we might, sometimes our care for a houseplant does not go well. Most problems are apparent in the leaves—they may change color, weaken, or even fall off. When a plant is looking unhappy, we must first consider whether there have been recent changes in its location or care. The problem may have various causes. To track it down, we should proceed step by step. Making several changes at once can harm a plant. Having said that, certain changes are unavoidable: a plant, like every other living organism, is subject to aging.

The table on the right will help you establish what is bothering your plant, and the numbers will lead you to a solution.

If you notice a problem, think about when you last watered, fertilized, repotted, and/or relocated your plant.

·····································

Study the leaves and substrate closely. The plant may be infested with pests.

·····································

Each problem could have multiple causes.

paling and withering
of leaves

dry tips

browning of
leaves

plant not
growing

yellowing of
leaves

leaf fall

curling
of leaves

spotting
on leaves

What trouble does your houseplant have?

	1	2	3	4	5	6	7	8	9	10	11
browning of leaves		●				●		●			
yellowing of leaves						●				●	
leaf fall		●			●	●	●	●		●	
paling and withering of leaves		●	●	●		●					●
curling of leaves					●	●				●	
spotting on leaves		●	●			●					●
dry tips		●	●		●	●	●		●	●	
plant not growing	●			●							

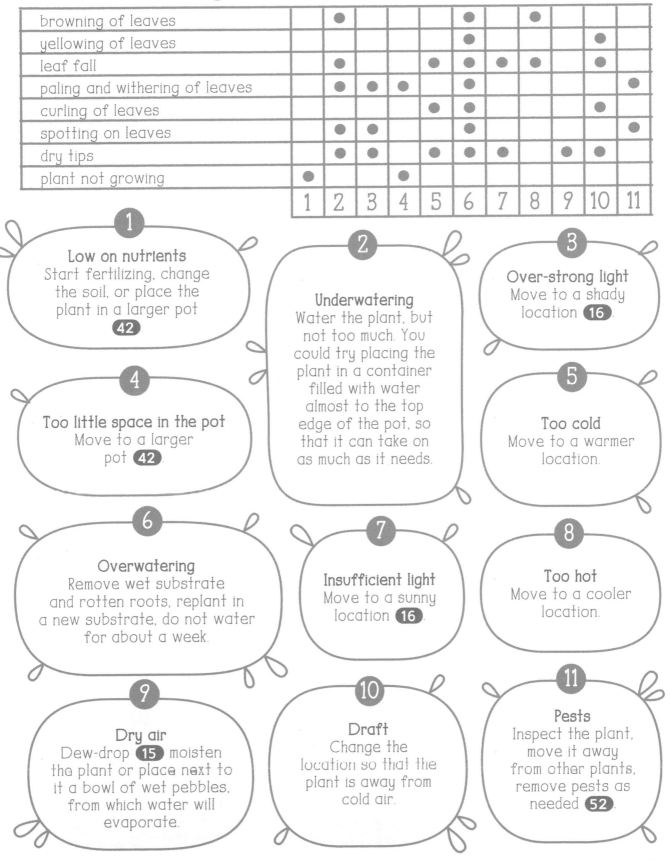

1
Low on nutrients
Start fertilizing, change the soil, or place the plant in a larger pot **42**

2
Underwatering
Water the plant, but not too much. You could try placing the plant in a container filled with water almost to the top edge of the pot, so that it can take on as much as it needs.

3
Over-strong light
Move to a shady location **16**.

4
Too little space in the pot
Move to a larger pot **42**.

5
Too cold
Move to a warmer location.

6
Overwatering
Remove wet substrate and rotten roots, replant in a new substrate, do not water for about a week.

7
Insufficient light
Move to a sunny location **16**.

8
Too hot
Move to a cooler location.

9
Dry air
Dew-drop **15** moisten the plant or place next to it a bowl of wet pebbles, from which water will evaporate.

10
Draft
Change the location so that the plant is away from cold air.

11
Pests
Inspect the plant, move it away from other plants, remove pests as needed **52**.

Pests

Houseplants and their substrate attract all kinds of pests. That's just how it is with plants. If your plant suddenly starts to wilt, it may have been attacked by tiny beetles. So if you discover these, do not hesitate to do battle with them. Pests can prevent a plant from growing and can infest other plants in the vicinity. In the fight against pests, perseverance is key, as is an ability to identify different pests and react accordingly.

Aphids

👁 Leaves are sticky and covered with black or gray patches. They may also be slightly misshapen.

✚ Shower the plant thoroughly and apply a special anti-aphid spray.

Scale bugs

👁 There are brown bulges on the leaves and stem. The leaves are sticky.

✚ Wipe bugs or entire infected leaves with an ethyl alcohol. A few days later, shower the plant. So the bug won't reappear, pour a special anti-scale-bug agent into the substrate.

Check your plants regularly and remove dry or damaged parts, which pests like to exploit.

If you find a pest on a plant, move this plant away from others before treating it.

Showers and soapsuds work very well on all pests, with the exception of sciaras. Soap each leaf thoroughly before rinsing with water at room temperature.

If there are quite a lot of pests, your only option is to use a special spray. These come in chemical and non-chemical types. Your choice depends on the pest in question, as different things work on different pests.

Spider mites

👁 Leaves shrivel and develop small light spots. Severe infestation forms a cobweb on the undersides of leaves or around the whole plant.

✚ Apply an anti-spider-mite spray then cover the plant with a plastic bag sealed at the bottom. A week later, remove the plant and air it out. Shower and dew-drop moisten regularly.

Thrips

👁 There are pale spots and patches on the leaves. The plant grows slowly, and new leaves are misshapen.

✚ Wash the whole plant with soap before treating it with an anti-thrip spray. Apply this spray repeatedly and use different types, as thrips adapt quickly to each spray and become resistant to it.

Sciaras

👁 The plant turns yellow and withers, and there are small black flies around it.

✚ Allow the substrate and plant to dry out thoroughly: scarias do not like dryness. Sprinkle sand on the surface of the substrate to ensure that the flies cannot fly out.

You're a proper carer at last!

So, that's about it from us! You're a houseplant cultivator. Your home is lovely and green. Your plants are thriving, and you can manage their every whim. But don't get to thinking that things are about to turn boring—plenty of challenges remain.

Try out new things from time to time. As a plant that needs moister air enjoys dew-drop moistening, it may also enjoy the humidifying effect of wet pebbles in its pot. Why not place a heat-loving plant in a small greenhouse, where it will happily cope with the fluctuating temperatures of winter?

Don't be afraid to experiment. Not all houseplants must be kept in a pot. Succulents, for instance, will thrive in an attractive glass terrarium. Other houseplants can be planted in a hanging ball of soil covered with moss, known as a *kokedama*, or even in a nutrient-rich aqueous solution. You can also shape your houseplants.

Don't lose your resolve. If your houseplant fails to thrive or dies, don't lose heart. Unfortunately, such things happen even to the most seasoned cultivators. Keeping houseplants is a learning curve for everyone. Don't be afraid to ask someone more experienced for help. Tips gleaned from practice are always the most valuable. And sometimes they come with cuttings that will grow into new plants!

Improve your skills. Try growing more demanding houseplants. Learn the plant-raising skills that this book doesn't have space to discuss. Did you know, for instance, that an avocado plant can be grown at home from its seed? And that palms can be propagated from seeds?

Above all, spread **the joy that growing houseplants gives**. Give a plant you have propagated to someone close to you, adding a few grower's tips for good measure.

Sources. Beyond our experiences, we have drawn on the following Czech sources: Pokojovky (www.pokojovky.co), Kvítka v bytě (www.kvitkavbyte.cz), and Zahrada na niti (zahradananiti.blogspot.com).

Here's wishing you the greatest success!

For more info, check out the following websites:

The Houseplant Guru
(thehouseplantguru.com)

Invincible Houseplants
(invinciblehouseplants.com)

Our House Plants
(www.ourhouseplants.com/)

© B4U Publishing for Albatros, an imprint of Albatros Media Group, 2023
5. května 1746/22, Prague 4, Czech Republic
Authors: Magda Garguláková, Lenka Chytilová
Illustrations @ Hannah Abbo
Translator: Andrew Oakland
Editor: Scott Alexander Jones

Printed in China by Leo Paper Group